Spiritual Life for Man

By Annie Besant

Copyright © 2021 Lamp of Trismegistus. All rights reserved. No part of this publication may be reproduced or transmitted in any form or by any means, electronic or mechanical, including photocopying, recording, or by any information storage and retrieval system, without permission in writing from Lamp of Trismegistus. Reviewers may quote brief passages.

ISBN: 978-1-63118-573-1

Esoteric Classics

Other Books in this Series and Related Titles

Aurora of the Philosophers by Paracelsus (978-1-63118-507-6)

Clairvoyance and Psychic Abilities by A Besant &c (978-1-63118-403-1)

The Feminine Occult by various authors (978-1-63118-711-7)

Rosicrucian Rules, Secret Signs, Codes and Symbols by various (978-1-63118-488-8)

An Outline of Theosophy by C W Leadbeater (978-1-63118-452-9)

Paracelsus, the Four Elements and Their Spirits by M P Hall (978-1-63118-400-0)

Essays on Ancient Magic by Helena P Blavatsky (978-1-63118-535-9)

Essays on the Esoteric Tradition of Karma by A Besant &c (978-1-63118-426-0)

The Use of Evil by Annie Besant (978-1-63118-532-8)

The Alchemical Catechism of Paracelsus by Paracelsus (978-1-63118-513-7)

Alchemy in the Nineteenth Century by Helena P Blavatsky (978-1-63118-446-8)

Qabbalistic Teachings and the Tree of Life by M P Hall (978-1-63118-482-6)

The Historic, Mythic and Mystic Christ by Annie Besant (978–1–63118–533–5)

The Hidden Mysteries of Christianity by Annie Besant (978–1–63118–534–2)

History, Analysis and Secret Tradition of the Tarot by Hall &c (978-1-63118-445-1)

Crystal Vision Through Crystal Gazing by Frater Achad (978-1-63118-455-0)

The Golden Verses of Pythagoras: Five Translations (978-1-63118-479-6)

Arcane Formulas or Mental Alchemy by W W Atkinson (978-1-63118-459-8)

The Machinery of the Mind by Dion Fortune (978-1-63118-451-2)

The A E Waite Reader: A Selection of Occult Essays (978-1-63118-515-1)

The Leadbeater Reader: A Selection of Occult Essays (978-1-63118-483-3)

Audio versions are also available on Audible, Amazon and Apple

Other Books in this Series and Related Titles

The Mysteries by Annie Besant (978–1–63118–572–4)

Fundamental Ideas of Theosophy by Bhagwan Das (978–1–63118–571–7)

Dreams: What They Are and How They Are Caused (978–1–63118–570–0)

Communication Between Different Worlds by Annie Besant (978–1–63118–569–4)

Animism, Magic and the Omnipotence of Thought by S Freud (978–1–63118–568–7)

Buddhism by F Otto Schrader (978–1–63118–567–0)

Death by W W Westcott (978–1–63118–566–3)

The Religion of Theosophy by Bhagwan Das (978–1–63118–565–6)

The Spirit of Zoroastrianism by Henry S Olcott (978–1–63118–564–9)

The Brotherhood of Religions by Annie Besant (978–1–63118–563–2)

Fourth Book of Maccabees by Josephus (978-1-63118-562-5)

The Story of Ahikar by Ahiqar (978-1-63118-561-8)

Vision of the Spirit by C. Jinarajadasa (978-1-63118-560-1)

Occult Arts by William Q. Judge (978-1-63118-559-5)

Kali the Mother by Sister Nivedita (978-1-63118-558-8)

Love and Death by Sri Aurobindo (978–1–63118–557–1)

Times and Seasons Volume 1, Numbers 4-6 (978-1-63118-556-4)

The Book of John Whitmer by John Whitmer (978-1-63118-554-0)

Interesting Account of Several Remarkable Visions (978-1-63118-553-3)

The Evening and Morning Star Volume 1, Numbers 11 & 12 (978-1-63118-552-6)

Private Diary of Joseph Smith 1832-1834 (978-1-63118-546-5)

Audio versions are also available on Audible, Amazon and Apple

Table of Contents

Introduction...7

Spiritual Life for the Man of the World...9

A Word on Man, His Nature and His Powers...25

INTRODUCTION

The word "esoteric" can be difficult to define. Esotericism in general can be seen less as a system of beliefs and more as a category, which encompasses numerous, different systems of beliefs. It's a bit of juxtaposition, since the word "esoteric" indicates something that few people know about, while the term itself broadly covers numerous philosophies, practices, areas of study and belief systems.

In a greater sense, Esotericism acts as a storehouse for secret knowledge, which is often considered ancient (by *tradition, if not by fact),* passed down from generation to generation, in private. At various times in history, simply possessing the knowledge of some of these subjects, was considered illegal and a jailable offence, if discovered. This usually included such general topics as Alchemy, Pharmacology, Qabalah, Hermeticism, Occultism, Ceremonial Magic, Astrology, Divination, Rosicrucianism and so on. Collectively, these areas of study were often referred to as the esoteric sciences.

Sometimes, the outer garment of a subject isn't esoteric, while what is hidden beneath it, is. As an example, Freemasonry isn't necessarily esoteric by nature (at *least not anymore),* but certain signs, passwords and handshakes given to the candidate during their initiation, are in fact, esoteric, in the sense that they are hidden from the general public.

Today, in the twenty-first century, such topics are readily available at bookstores across the country, and numerous mainsteam publishers offer beginners guides and coffee-table volumes on many of these subjects, intended for mass appeal. Books like *"The Secret"* have turned previously arcane topics into household knowledge. All that being the case, however, it isn't to say that there still aren't buried secrets to uncover, ancient wisdom being ignored and forgotten mysteries to be explored. In fact, it is often that we are only able to further our own studies by standing on the shoulders of these disappearing giants.

Lamp of Trismegistus is doing its part to help preserve humanity's esoteric history by making some of these classics available to those students who are seeking to unearth the knowledge of these ancient colossi.

So, be sure to check other titles from our *Esoteric Classics* series, as well as our *Occult Fiction, Theosophical Classics, Foundations of Freemasonry Series, Supernatural Fiction, Paranormal Research Series, Studies in Buddhism* and our *Christian Apocrypha Series.* You can also download the audio versions of most of these titles from Amazon, Apple or Audible, for learning on the go.

SPIRITUAL LIFE FOR THE MAN OF THE WORLD

The Rev. R. J. Campbell, M.A., who presided, said: In introducing the lecturer to a City Temple audience it is not my desire to indulge in personalities which might be embarrassing to her, but I feel it is due to ourselves to say that we recognize in Mrs. Besant one of the greatest moral forces of the day. She has well earned the respect now so freely accorded to her by the British public, and by many thousands of thoughtful men and women all over the world. In time past she has had to sacrifice much for her fidelity to what she believed to be the truth. It is rare in such a case that strength of conviction is untainted by any trace of bitterness or intolerance. In proportion to the price that has had to be paid for one's convictions is the intensity and, sometimes shall we say, the dogmatism, and even intolerance, with which they are held; but if there is one outstanding characteristic of Mrs. Besant's public life it is the entire absence of any trace either of bitterness or intolerance in her dealings with others. She looks for truth beneath all formal statements of belief; she excommunicates no one; and, therefore, as her acquaintance with life is so wide and deep, she has earned the position of a great spiritual teacher, and it is as such that we welcome her to the City Temple tonight.

Before beginning that which I am to say to you tonight, will you permit me one word of preface both on my presence here and on the opinions which here I shall voice. I thank your minister and I thank you for giving me the opportunity of speaking here, but l am bound to say that the opinions I give must not be taken in any way to compromise the place in which I speak, or the minister who generally occupies this pulpit. We are all grateful to the minister of the City Temple for the courage with which he has given utterance to opinions which are in the air for educated and thoughtful people, but which only the few have the courage to express. But when a truth is in the air the expression of that truth is one of the greatest services that man can render to man: for truth, you must remember, is largely dependent upon the utterance of those who see it and are brave enough to speak it, and thousands welcome a truth that they know to be true, but have not the courage to speak it out while speech is still confined to the minority. It is therefore the more important that I may not be held in anything I say to compromise in any fashion the message which here is normally delivered. For my opinions are mine, as yours are yours, and in speaking here tonight I speak the truth as I see it, not desiring that any shall accept it who as yet see it not, and least of all desiring that any word of mine shall render heavier the burden or greater the difficulty which you (turning to Mr. Campbell), Sir, have to face.

Now the complaint which we hear continually from thoughtful and earnest-minded people, a complaint against the circumstances of their life, is perhaps one of the most fatal. "If my circumstances were different from what they are, how much more I could do; if only I were not so surrounded by business, so tied by anxieties and cares, so occupied with the work of the world, then I would be able to live a more spiritual life". Now that is not true. No circumstances can ever make or mar the unfolding of the spiritual life in man. Spirituality does not depend upon the environment; it depends upon the attitude of the man towards life, and I want if I can tonight to point out to you the way in which the world may be turned to the service of the Spirit instead of submerging it, as I admit it often does. If a man does not understand the relation of the material and the spiritual; if he separates off the one from the other as incompatible and hostile; if on the one side he puts the life of the world, and on the other the life of the Spirit as rivals, as antagonists, as enemies, the one of the other, then the pressing nature of worldly occupations, the powerful shocks of the material environment, the constant luring of physical temptation, and the occupying of the brain by physical cares — these things are apt to make the life of the Spirit unreal. They seem the only reality, and we have to find some alchemy, some magic, by which the life of the world shall be seen to be the unreal, and the life of the Spirit the only reality. If we can do that, then the reality will express itself through the life of the world, and that life will become its means of expression, and not a bandage round its eyes, a gag which stops the breath. That is what we are to seek for tonight.

Now, you know how often in the past this question, whether a man can lead a spiritual life in the world, has been answered in the negative. In every land, in every religion, in every age of the world's history, when the question has been asked, the answer has been: "No, the man of the world cannot lead a spiritual life". That answer comes from the deserts of Egypt, the jungles of India, the monastery and the nunnery in Roman Catholic countries, in every land and place where man has sought to find out God by shrinking from the company of men; and if for the knowledge of God and the leading of the spiritual life it be necessary to fly from the haunts of men, then that life for the most of us is impossible, for we are bound by circumstance that we cannot break to live the life of the world and to accommodate ourselves to its conditions. I am going to submit to you that that idea is based on a fundamental error, but that it is largely fostered in our modern life, not so much so in this country by thinking of secluded life in jungle or desert, in cave or monastery, but rather by thinking that the religious and the secular must be kept apart. That is a tendency here because of the modern way of separating what is called the sacred from that which is called the profane. People here speak of Sunday as the Lord's Day, as though every day were not His equally, and He should be served on it. To call one day the Lord's day is to deny that same lordship to every other day in the week, and so make six parts of the life outside the spiritual, while only one remains recognized as dedicated to the Spirit. And so the common talk of men — sacred history and profane history, religious education and secular education — all these phrases that are so commonly used, they hypnotise the public mind into a false view of the Spirit and the world. The right way is to say that the Spirit is the life, the world the form, and the form must be the expression of the life, otherwise you have a corpse devoid of life, and you have an unembodied life, separated from all means of effective action; and I want to put broad and strong the very foundation of what I believe to be all right and sane thinking in this matter. The world is the thought of God, the expression of the Divine Mind. All useful activities are forms of Divine activity. The wheels of the world are turned by God, and men are only His hands which touch the rim of the wheel. All work done in the world is God's work, or none is His at all. Everything that serves man and helps on the activities of the world is rightly seen when seen as a Divine activity, and wrongly seen when called secular or profane. The merchant in his counting-house, the shopman behind his counter, the doctor in the hospital, is quite as much engaged in a Divine activity as any preacher in his church. Until that is realised the world is vulgarised, and until we can see one life everywhere, and all things rooted in that life, until then it is we who are hopelessly profane in attitude, we who are blind to the Beatific Vision, which is the sight of the One Life in everything, and all things as expressions of that Life.

Now, if that be true, if there is only one life in which you and I are partakers, one creative thought by which the worlds were formed and are maintained, then, however mighty may be the unexpressed

Divine existence — though it be true as it is written in an ancient Indian Scripture, "I established this universe with one fragment of Myself, and I remain" — however true it may be that Divinity transcends the manifestation thereof, none the less the manifestation is still divine; and by understanding that we touch the feet of God. If it be true that He is everywhere and in everything, then He is as much in the market- place as in the desert, as much in the counting-house as in the jungle, as easily found in the street of the crowded city as in the solitude of the mountain peak. I do not mean that it is not easier for you and for me to realize the Divine greatness in the splendor, say, of snow-clad mountains, the beauty of some pine forest, the depth of some marvelous secret valley where Nature speaks in a voice that may be heard; but I do mean that although we hear more clearly there, it is because we are deaf, and not because the Divine voice does not speak. Ours the weakness, that the rush and the bustle of life in the city makes us deaf to the voice that is ever speaking; and if we were stronger, if our ears were keener, if we were more spiritual, then we could find the Divine life as readily in the rush of Holborn Viaduct as in the fairest scene that Nature has ever painted in the solitude of the mountain or the magic of the midnight sky. That is the first thing to realize — that we do not find because our eyes are blinded.

But now let us see what are the conditions by which the man of the world may lead the spiritual life, for I admit there are conditions. Have you ever asked yourselves why around you objects that attract you are found on every side, things you want to possess ? Your desires answer to the outer beauty, the attractiveness, of the endless objects that are scattered over the world. If they were not meant to attract they would not be there; if they were really hindrances, why should they have been put in our path ? Just for the same reason as when a mother wants to coax her child into the exertion that will induce it to walk she dangles before its eyes a little out of reach some dazzling toy, some tinsel attraction, and the child's eyes are gained by the brilliant object, and the child wants to grasp the thing just out of its reach. He tries to get on his feet, falls, and rises again, endeavors to walk, struggles to reach, and the value of the attraction is not in the tinsel that presently the child grasps, crushes, and throws away, wanting something more, but in the stimulus to the life within which makes him endeavor to move in order to gain the glittering prize that he despises when he has won it. And the great mother-heart, by which we are trained, is ever dangling in front of us some attractive object, some prize for the child-spirit, turning outwards the powers that live within; and in order to induce exertion, in order to win to the effort by which alone those inward-turned powers will turn outwards into manifestation, we are bribed and coaxed and induced to make efforts by the endless toys of life scattered on every side. We struggle, we endeavor to grasp; at last we do grasp and hold; after a short time the brilliant apple turns to ashes, as in Milton's fable, and the prize that seemed so valuable loses all its attractiveness, becomes worthless, and something else is desired. In that way we grow. The result is in ourselves; some power has been brought out, some faculty has been developed, some inner strength has become a manifested power, some hidden capacity has become faculty in action. That is the object of the Divine teacher; the toy is thrown aside when the result of the exertion to gain it has been achieved. And so we pass from one point to another, so we pass from one stage of evolution to the next; and although until you believe in the great fact of continual rebirth and ever-continuing experience, you will not realize to the full the beauty and the splendor of the Divine plan, still, even in one brief life you know you gain by your struggle and not by your accomplishment, and the reward of the struggle is in the power that you possess, or, in the great words of Carpenter, narrowed down if you do not believe in reincarnation: "Every pain that I suffered in one body was a power that I wielded in the next". And even in one life you can see it, even in one brief span from the cradle to the grave you can trace the working of the law. You grow, not by what you gain of outer fruit, but by the inner unfolding necessary for your success in the struggle.

Now, if long natural experience has made wise the man, these objects lose their power to attract, and the first tendency then is to cease from effort; but that would mean stagnation. When the objects of the world are becoming a little less valuable than they were, then is the time to look for some new motive, and the motive to action for the spiritual life is, first, to perform action because it is duty, and not in order to gain the personal reward that it may bring. Let me take the case of a man of the world and a spiritual man, and see what it needs to turn one into the other. I take one in which you will not question that he is a man of the world, a man who is making some enormous fortune, who puts before himself as the one object of life money, to be rich. It is a common thing. Now, for a moment, pause on the life of the man who has determined to be rich. Everything is subordinated to that one aim. He must be master of his body, for if that body is his master he will waste with every week and month the money that he has gathered by struggle; he will waste in luxury for the pleasing of the body the money that he ought to grip, in order that he may win more. And so the first thing that a man must do is to master the body, to teach it to endure hardness, to learn to bear frugality, to learn to bear hardship even; not to think whether he wants to sleep, if by traveling all night a contract can be gained; not to stop to ask whether he shall rest if, by going to some party at midnight, he can make a friend who will enable him to gain more money by his influence. Over and over again in the struggle for gold the man must be master of this outer body that he wears, until it has no voice in determining his line of activity — it yields itself obedient servant to the dominant will, to the compelling brain. That is the first thing he learns — conquest of the body.

Then he learns concentration of mind. If he is not concentrated, his rivals will beat him in the struggle of the market-place. If his mind wanders about here, there, and everywhere, undecided, one day trying one plan, and another day another plan, without perseverance, without deliberate continuing labor, that man will fail. The goal he desires teaches him to concentrate his mind; he brings it to one point; he holds it there as long as he needs it; he is steady in his persevering mental effort, and his mind grows stronger and stronger, keener and keener, more and more under his control. He has not only learned to control his body, but to control his mind. Has he gained anything more ? Yes, a strong will; only the strong will can succeed in such a struggle. The soul grows mighty in the attempt to achieve. Presently that man, with his mastered body, his well-controlled mind, his powerful will, gains his objects and grasps his gold. And, then ? Then he finds out that, after all, he cannot do so very much with it to make happiness for himself; that he has only got one body to clothe, one mouth to feed; that he cannot multiply his wants with the enormous supply that he can gain, and that, after all, his happiness-gaining power is very limited. His gold becomes a burden rather than a joy, the first delight of the achievement of his object palls, and he becomes satiated with possession, until in many a case, he can do nothing but, by mere habit, roll and roll and roll up increasing piles of useless gold. It becomes a nightmare rather than a delight; it crushes the man who won it.

Now, what will make that man a spiritual man ? A change of his object — that is all. Let that man in this or any other life awaken to the valuelessness of the gold that he has heaped together: let him see the beauty of human service; let him catch a glimpse of the splendor of the Divine order; let him realize that all that life is worth is to give it as part of the great life by which the worlds are maintained, and the power he has gained over body, over mind, over will, will make that man a giant in the spiritual world. He does not need to change those qualities but to get rid of the selfishness, to get rid of the indifference to human pain, to get rid of the recklessness with which he crushed his brother, in order that he might climb into wealth on the starvation of myriads. He must change his ideal from selfishness to service; from strength used for crushing to strength used for uplifting; and in the giant of the money market you will have the spiritual man; his life is consecrated to humanity, and he owns no duty save to serve and to help. Difference of object, difference of motive, not difference of the outer, on that does it depend whether a man is of the world worldly or of the Spirit spiritual.

I used just now the word duty, for that is the first step. Any one of you, whatever may be your work in the world, it matters not, if you begin to do it not because it brings you a livelihood — though there is nothing to be ashamed of in its bringing you the power to live here — if you begin to do it slowly, gradually, more and more because it ought to be done, and not because you want to gain something for yourself, then you are taking the first step towards the spiritual life, you are changing your motive; all the activities of your day will have a new object. Duty must be done; the wheels of the world must be kept turning. Men and women must be fed along the various lines of trade and commerce; the sick must be healed; the ignorant must be taught; justice must be sought as between the strong and the weak, the rich and the poor; and, looking at it thus, the tradesman, the merchant, the doctor, the lawyer, the teacher may all take a new view of life, and that they may say: "This activity with which I am engaged is part of the great working of the world which is Divine. I am in it to do it, and my duty lies in the perfect performance of my task. I will teach, or heal, or argue, or trade, or enter into commercial relations of all kinds, not for the mere money that it brings, or the power that it yields, but in order that the great work of the world may be worthily carried on, and that work may be done by me as servant of a Will greater than my own, instead of for my own personal gain and profit".

That is the first step, and there is not one of you that cannot take it. You may do your business just the same, but you carry a new spirit with you into it; you do it because it is your work in the world, as a servant does a task for his master because he is bidden to do it, and his loyalty makes him do it well. Then every adding up of a number of figures in a ledger, every selling of an article in a shop would be done with this sublime ideal behind it: "I do it as a part of the world's work, and this is the duty that falls to my lot to do" and would be taken as coming directly from the great Will by which the worlds move, as your share of the Divine activity, your part of the universal work; and the mightiest Archangel, the greatest of the Shining Ones, can do nothing more than his share of carrying out the Divine Will. And George Herbert wrote truly that the one who sweeps a room as to the glory of God makes that and the action fine. That is spiritual life where all is done for duty, for the larger instead of for the smaller self. And mind, it is not always easy. No shuffling, no leaving of a task undone, because the Master's eye will not be there, for our Master's eye is everywhere, and never sleeping. No scamping of work, for that is not to be one of the Divine artificers, but only an ignorant and clumsy worker. Art is only doing what you do perfectly, and God is always an artist. There is nothing, however small, no animal that only the microscope enables you to see, that is not perfect in its beauty, and the more closely you examine the more exquisite does it become. Why, those minute diatoms that you can only see by the microscope, every minute shell is sculptured with patterns geometrically perfect — for whom ? For the satisfaction of that sense of perfection which is one of the Divine elements in God and man alike. Not what you do, but how you do it, whether it be perfectly wrought to the utmost limit of your ability; that is the test of a man's character, and by the work you can know the character of the worker.

Now that seems a small thing when you bring it down to your own house, shop, office. Taken one by one, so small; but suppose every one did it, how would the face of the world then appear ? No scamped work, no unreliable products on the market, nothing adulterated, nothing that was not what it pretended to be, the face value and the real value always identical, every house perfectly built, every drain perfectly laid, everything done as well as the skill and strength of man can do it. Why, a world like that seems a fairy tale, an impossible Utopia, but that would be the result if every individual man did his duty as perfectly as his powers permitted. And that is the first step towards the spiritual life. It is not outside your reach; it is close to every one of you.

But that is not all; there is a higher stage of the spiritual life than that. It is much to feel yourself co-worker with the Divine in the world, much to make your work great by knitting it to the universal work throughout this mighty system of worlds and universes; much, too, as Emerson said, to hitch your wagon to a star, instead of some miserable post by the wayside. But even that is not the only thing within your powers, even that is not the most splendid to which you can attain. For there is one thing greater even than duty, and that is when all action is done as sacrifice. Now, what does that mean ? There would be no world, no you, no I, if there had not been a primary sacrifice by which a fragment of the Divine Thought sheathed itself in matter, limited itself in order that you and I might become self-consciously Divine. There is a profound truth in that great Christian teaching of a Lamb slain — when ? On Calvary ? No, "from the foundation of the world". That is the great truth of sacrifice. No Divine Sacrifice, no universe. No Divine Self-limitations, none of the worlds which fill the realms of space. It is all a sacrifice, the sacrifice of love that limits itself that others may gain self-conscious being and rejoice in the perfection of their own ultimate Divinity. And inasmuch as the life of the world is based on sacrifice, all true life is also sacrificial; and when every action is done as sacrifice then the man becomes the perfect, spiritual man. Now that is hard. The first stage is not so difficult. We may give away largely; we may make our lives useful; but how difficult it is when, our lives being made useful, and wrapped up in some useful work, to be able to see that work shivered into pieces, and look on its ruins with calm content. That is one of the things that is meant by sacrifice — that you may throw the whole of your life into some good work, the whole of your energy into some great scheme, you may toil and build and plan and shape, and you may nourish your own begotten scheme as a mother may cherish the child of her womb, and presently it falls to pieces round you. It fails, it does not succeed; it breaks, it does not grow; it dies, it does not live. Can you be content with such a result ? Years of labor, years of thought, years of sacrifice, and see everything crumble into dust, and nothing remain ? If not, then you are working for self, and not as part of the Divine activity; and however gilded over with love of others your scheme may have been, it was your work and not God's work, and therefore you have suffered in the breaking. For if it were really His and not yours, if it were a sacrifice and not your own possession, you would know that all that is good in it must inevitably go into the forces of good in the world, and that if He did not want the form you built, you would rather it were broken and the life that cannot die go into other forms which fit better with the Divine plan and work into the great scheme of evolution.

Let me put it another way, and you will see exactly what I mean, less abstractly perhaps. Take an army, waiting attack from some enemy greater, stronger than itself. The commander-in-chief maps out his scheme of battle, places one regiment in one spot and one regiment in another, makes one great plan that includes the whole, and the day of battle dawns. From the side of the general goes a galloping messenger, and he sends word to some young captain in one part of the field: "Go, attack that fort that lies in front of you, capture it, and hold it until word comes to leave". And the young captain, with his little band of young men behind him, looks at the fort in front, and knows he cannot take it, sees that failure is inevitable, knows that it means mutilation and death to the men under his command — nay, he knows that if he carries out the order to the last, not one man of that little band may see tomorrow's sun, but every one will be swept away in the death hail that will come upon them as they struggle up the hill to the impregnable fort at the top. He sees it all; does he hesitate ? If he does he is traitor, dishonored, craven. He calls his men together. "Orders have come to take the fort !" They charge up at it. They are decimated. Again they charge, and again they leave a tenth of their number on the slope. Again, and again, and again they charge, until no man is left there to stand and charge again. Meanwhile, on another side of the field progress has been made with the general's plan; meanwhile the attention of the enemy has been occupied by this handful of men who go cheerfully to death, and the plan has developed; for while the enemy were watching the forlorn hope, the plan of their comrades has been carried out on the other side, and in the long run, when the sun is setting, victory belongs to the army, although those men lie spread dead and dying on the slope. Have they failed

? It looks like failure to lie there dying and dead; surely the men have failed. Ah ! when the story of that battle is written, when a grateful nation raises a monument to the memory of the conquerors of that battle, high on that monument will be graven in imperishable gold the names of the men who died and made victory possible for their comrades by accepting defeat for themselves.

You read my parable. There is no failure where the commander-in-chief is the Divine Architect of the universe, no failure, but inevitable success; and shall it not be a pride to anyone who is called to sacrifice in order that the plan may be carried out ? And there is no failure, for victory is ever on the Divine side. What matters it if you and I look like failures; what matters it if our petty plans crumble to pieces in our hands; what matters it if our schemes of a moment are found to be useless and are thrown aside?

The life we have thrown into them, the devotion with which we planned them, the strength with which we strove to carry them out, the sacrifice with which we offered them to the success of the mighty whole, that enrolled us as sacrificial workers with Deity, and no glory is greater than the glory of the personal failure which ensures universal success. That is only for the strong. I grant it. That is only for the heroes. It is their work and their delight. But even to be able to see the beauty of it is to bring some of the beauty into every one of our lives. For to see a thing to be noble is to begin to incarnate that nobility in your life, and the mere recognition of the splendor of an ideal is the first step towards becoming transformed into its image.

Now suppose that you and I can shape our lives on lines such as these which inadequately I have tried to sketch, we shall become the spiritual man living in the life of the world, making the world slowly after the fashion of the Divine ideal, and making it more and more the perfectly manifested Divine thought. That, is the central idea then which will transform the man of the world into the spiritual man, and in the world it can best be performed. The life of the jungle, for those who know the many lives of men, is never the last life of a savior of his race. Sometimes such a life will be one of the many lives through which he goes to gather universal experience; sometimes a time of gathering strength together and accumulating the power that hereafter is to be used; but the life of the Christs of the race is the life in the world, and not the life in the jungle. Though we may profitably go sometimes into seclusion, the manifested God walks in the haunts of men. For only there is the great work to be done, there the trials to be faced, there the powers to be opened up. When all our powers are brought out, when we are all of us Christs, ah ! then we can go out of the outer life of the world to become part of its inner life which shapes and moulds the outer activity; but those who are only growing to that stature must grow by the law of growth, and that is the law of experience. But only the perfect may pass behind the veil and thence send out the spiritual powers unfolded in the life of the world.

And so it seems to me there is not one of us who may not begin to lead the truly spiritual life, and the world will be the better for the living, while the man will unfold the more rapidly for his effort. For every one of us, if we only think of it, each one is at work to carve his own life into a perfect image, the image of the Divine manifest in man. It is not that the Divine is not within you; were it not so, how should you bring it forth ? The ideal comes before the manifestation, the thought creates the form, and in every one of you there is sleeping, as it were, the Divine image, and your work is to make that image manifest, and then you are the spiritual man. Come with me to the studio of some great sculptor, not a mere marble-chipper, but one of those geniuses who show the marble living, and the ideal in spotless form. How does that man work? Do you think he is carving a statue out of the marble? He is doing nothing of the kind. He is setting free a statue within the marble, and cutting away the superincumbent, useless marble that hides from the eyes of man the beauty of the ideal that he sees. That is the sculptor of genius; in the rough block, which is all that you and I can see with our poor eyes, he sees the perfect statue imprisoned within the stone, and with every blow of mallet, and with every deft touch of chisel, he brings that prisoner nearer to freedom, his ideal nearer to manifestation. And so with you and with me: we are rough blocks of marble as we live here in the studio of the world, rough, unhewn, so many of us, and the Divinity within us is hidden, as the statue within the block. And you and I are sculptors, and by our life that statue is to be made manifest, that imprisoned beauty is to be set free, and with the mallet of will, the chisel of thought, we must cut away all this superincumbent, useless stone that hides the living Divinity within us, hides its unmanifested glory from the sight of men. Sculptors every one of you, shaping out what you shall inevitably be in years, in centuries, to come, and the more skillfully, with the more knowledge, with the stronger will, the more powerfully you can use your mallet and your chisel, the swifter will come the day of liberation, the nearer the manifestation of the work. And so, wherever you may be, in whatever workshop of this great world you may find yourselves at labor, keep ever in your heart the ideal that you fain would realize. Feel the presence of the imprisoned Divinity that you have the mighty privilege, and you alone, of liberating; and take in hand your tools, cut away the worthless stone, liberate the splendid statue, and then you shall know yourself self-consciously as that which you really are, men in the image of God.

A WORD ON MAN, HIS NATURE AND HIS POWERS

A Lecture delivered on board the "Kaiser-Hind" in the Red Sea, October 30th, 1893

I propose to put before you what the esoteric philosophy teaches concerning man: man's nature and man's powers, his possibilities in the future, as well as his state in the present. May I say in opening what I have to put to you, that I am simply laying before you that which I have been taught, and which I have to a considerable extent verified by my own personal experiment, so that it has become to me a matter of knowledge ? I, however, only put it to you as a matter of reasonable hypothesis. I do not pretend to dictate to you your opinions; I do not pretend to formulate for you what you shall think, or what you shall reject. On each of you the responsibility of forming his own thought; on each of you the responsibility of accepting or rejecting, as your own reason, your conscience and your judgment may decide. All that the speaker can do, or has the right to do, is to put the truth as he sees it, leaving it to each individual to accept or to reject, the right and the duty being on each, and not on the one who speaks.

With regard to man, there is a fundamental difference in the conception of man as he is looked at in the East and the West. According to the esoteric philosophy man is regarded essentially as a soul. What he may have of instruments which that soul employs, what bodies he may clothe himself in, what special forms he may adopt — all that is matter which changes in time and space. As you may read in *The Brihad Aranyaka Upanishat* "As a goldsmith, taking a piece of gold, forms another shape ... so throwing off this body ... the soul forms a shape". And so the man is the soul, the soul that lives to gather experience, that lives to subjugate external nature, that lives to unite itself with the Divine Spirit whence it sprang; and as regards the soul's bodies, those differ as evolution proceeds, and the soul moulds them century after century into the fuller and more perfect expression of itself. But in the West, man is far more identified with his outer form; he identifies himself with his body and with his mind. To us the soul stands above body and mind, using both as instruments, whereas in the West, people think of themselves as consisting of body and of mind; and the things that interest them are the things that affect the body, while the mind, they think, is practically their master, and they never dream of mastering their own thoughts and being ruler of their own intellectual as well as of their own physical domain.

In order that these distinctions may be understood, let us sketch the different "principles" as they are sometimes called — "states of consciousness" as they are called at other times — which make up man when, you take him completely, as man physical, man psychical, and man spiritual. Those are the three great divisions accepted, let me say in passing, by Christianity as much as by other religions. For you find St. Paul speaking of man "as body, soul and spirit". I know that in popular Christianity the distinction between soul and spirit has very largely been lost. But that is not so in Christian philosophy. If you take the writings of the great thinkers of Christendom, those who have dealt with religion scientifically and philosophically, you will find they follow the lines laid down by the great Christian Apostle, and regard man as a triple and not only as a dual entity. Now the body which belongs to the man, which is a physical garment as we say, is a very changing and a very illusory thing, as I said to you the other night, — changing continually from moment to moment, and from year to year; so that if you turn to any modern book on Physiology you will find that every minute particle of your body changes absolutely and completely in the space of seven years, that not a fragment of it you had seven years ago is yours today. Not only so. In the later investigations of Physiology you will find it recognised in the West, that a great part, at least, of the body, is made up of minute lives, microbes as they are called; and whenever men of science are searching after the cause of disease, they are on the track of some particular microbe, and it has become one of their favourite recreations to cultivate the microbe and improve him, so that he may become less dangerous when he falls upon any particular body. In this, western science is on the track of a great truth, and as far as it goes it speaks rightly in the fact that these microbes enter into the composition of the human body. It might go further: it might say that the whole body is made up of nothing else but microbes and minuter creatures still, so that the whole body of man is composed of tiny lives, lives each with its own independent existence, coming into the body and going out of it, taking while in the body the stamp of the individual man, of which, for a time, it forms a part. So that our bodies are like hosts of these tiny visitors, and each of us stamps on those particles of the body his own physical, and, to a great extent, his mental, moral, and emotional characteristics. Out of the great reservoir of nature, there pour through us these streams of tiny lives; and each, while it remains in our keeping, receives our stamp and then passes on to form part of some other body — vegetable, mineral, animal, human, as the case may be. So that even physically we become the creators of the world in which we live. Even physically, the world, as it surrounds us, is made up of that which we contribute, and is modified and changed according/ to the character of these constant contributions that we make. Into our body flow the tiny lives. There we feed them, poison them or purify them, pollute them or cleanse them, as the case may be. By our food and by our drink, by our thinking and by our living, we modify these tiny particles which are a passing part of ourselves ; and then we send them out to affect others — to make part of the bodies of other people, to make part of the physical nature around us, modifying them according to the fashion in which we are living ourselves. This is the physical basis of human brotherhood, this the physical basis of the brotherhood of all that lives. And there is nothing that lives not. So that this constant interaction throws on each a responsibility, gives to each the responsibility of this creative power, of this transmuting and modifying influence. One by one we change each other's lives physically, day by day we affect each other's health mentally as well as morally. Sometimes it is said that the man who is evil in his living, as the drunkard, is only his own enemy. It is not so. He is the enemy of everything that surrounds him, of every life that comes in contact with his own. The terrible curse of the drunkard is that all these tiny lives are sent out from him, poisoned with alcohol, to fall on the bodies of other men, women and children, carrying with them the poison that he has infused into them, and making him a focus of curses to all among whom he lives. Thus, learning what the physical body is, the esoteric philosophy makes us careful in our physical life. It carries on this sense of responsibility into the common actions, common thoughts of everyday and ordinary life, so that self-restraint in the body as well as in the mind, should be the note of the life of every true Theosophist.

Let me pass from the body to the next stage in man, that astral body to which I alluded the other night. Really the astral body should come first in our thought, for it is the stable matrix or mould, into which all these tiny physical lives pass, and out of which they pass again, the stable part of man which preserves the form, only slowly and gradually modified, which is more directly acted upon by the mind than the physical molecules, which affects the physical molecules in their arrangement, in that as you alter the matrix these physical molecules must take on the form of the mould into which they run. This astral body of astral matter envelopes every physical molecule, and not only envelopes every physical molecule, but spreads out around the body, making a kind of atmosphere around each of us, extending some few feet away on every side, so that a clairvoyant looking at the body sees the physical body surrounded by what is called an aura, that is, a vibrating mass of delicate matter, visible to any one who is sensitive under special conditions, but visible normally to the clairvoyant, and differing in appearance according to the state of health, physical, psychical or mental, of the person whom it concerns. Now, that aura, or atmosphere, surrounding the body, which is in a sense an expansion of astral matter, is very closely connected especially with the mind; it is very easily affected by the mind of the person to whom it belongs, and also by the minds of others. These magnetic atmospheres that surround us (for in astral matter all magnetic forces play) bring us into contact one with the other, so that we affect each other unconsciously, as we sometimes say. Have you never felt on meeting a person for the first time an attraction or a repulsion which had nothing in it of intellectual judgment, nothing in it of previous knowledge or experience ? You like a person — you cannot tell why; you dislike another — you have no reason for your dislike. Esoteric philosophy explains to you the very simple reason that causes these strange antipathies and attractions. It is that every human being has his own rate of vibration, the vibration of this astral matter, so that it is always quivering backwards and forwards. It is one of the characteristics of this ethereal matter to be thrown easily into waves; and just as light is nothing more than waves of ether set in very rapid motion by a rapidly vibrating body, which we call luminous, because of the effect it has upon the eye, so this ethereal matter, which is part of our own bodies, is thrown into waves of definite length and definite frequency and these vibrate always in us and around us, and are part of ourselves, modified by our own characteristics. Just as striking two strings on a piano, you may have either harmony or discord, according to the length of the sound-waves set up by these vibrating strings — so you may have either harmony or discord between the vibrating auras of two different people; and if the vibrations fall into harmony — that is, if they bear a certain definite relation of wave length to each other — there is an attraction between the two: whereas, if they bear a different relation you get discord — that is, friction and jangle, and you are repelled without understanding the reason.

It is this astral body and astral atmosphere which is the medium for all magnetic phenomena. All the effects we produce upon each other are modified by this astral atmosphere. All the effects that deal with emotions and passions, with all those sides of the human character which are of the nature of emotions, come to us by means of these astral vibrations.

Have you ever tried to think what oratory is? It does not lie in the words that are spoken, it does not lie in the thought that is behind the words. You might take in cold blood the most eloquent passage of some great oration, and read it calmly without any movement of the emotions, without any sense of passion or of vibrating enthusiasm in you. If you hear it spoken, it is different. Why? It is because the thought of the speaker working on his own astral atmosphere throws that into vehement vibrations — vibrations of love or of hatred, passion or pity — vibrations of great enthusiasm; and then these vibrations of his, throwing the whole ether around him into wave motion, these waves strike person after person, making their own atmosphere vibrate, and then from one to another there flies the contagion until the whole crowd is moved as by a single impulse and a single will.

These are all results of this second part of man's nature, this astral atmosphere that penetrates and surrounds him, by means of which the mind works on physical matter. And not only in this fashion, but in many forms of nervous disease, in those strange crises of panic, in those often puzzling attacks of hysterical affection that rush through a whole hospital. There you have set up these vibrations in the astral atmosphere communicated from patient to patient, and bringing about nervous crises in the physical body which they control.

With regard to this astral body and atmosphere, many investigations are being made in modern science, and many of our acutest thinkers are beginning to realise that it is necessary to postulate such a nature in man in order to explain many of the obscurer phenomena to which so much of our modern thought is directed. Into this part of man's nature fall all the phenomena of trance, all the lower phenomena of mesmerism, and many of the phenomena of hypnotism. Although mind comes into mesmeric and hypnotic phenomena, it works on the astral body of the person who is subject to the influence, and by producing effects in the astral body brings about results in the physical. Psychologists in the West — men like Sidgwick, Sully, Bain, and many another of our leading writers on psychology — have found that they cannot understand the workings of consciousness if they only study it in its waking state; that is, if they only study the mind as we know it in our waking hours, they meet with phenomena that are quite inexplicable, and they have begun to study sleep-consciousness — a very bad name for it but apparently there is no better at present in the English tongue — in order the better to understand the phenomena shown by the mind in its waking state. This sleep-consciousness includes all conditions of trance. There is this advantage of the trance condition — you can produce it at will; and every scientist will tell you that if he wants to gain exact facts, he needs to control his experiments, and to shut out what he does not want, to include only the conditions which he desires in order that he may make his experiments. The moment he can produce these special conditions he can work out all the facts he is in search of with less liability to error than would otherwise occur. By artificially including trance, human consciousness can be studied in a fashion which is normally impossible: trance is produced sometime by drugs, sometimes by mesmeric passes (that is, by the action of the mind and the will upon another) sometimes by hypnotism (that is, by using a mechanical stimulus like a revolving mirror or electric light) — there are many ways of doing it — fatiguing the external sense, so that the fatigue leads to paralysis of the cells of the nerve, and that paralysis is propagated backwards to the brain, producing ultimately a state of brain fatigue, brain paralysis, in fact a state of coma. In these fashions, man may be thrown into these abnormal states of consciousness, and studied when consciousness is working in this particular state instead of in the normal condition. In hypnotism these results are brought about mechanically. Mr. Braid, who first started these hypnotic experiments, brought them about by producing what he called a convergent strabismus. That is only a six-syllabled way of saying "a squint"; but sometimes the scientific mind likes to speak in six syllables rather than in one, because it produces a certain sense of dignity which impresses the unscientific and thoughtless. Really, what he did was to make the patient squint upwards by putting an object slightly above the eyes so that they had to converge in looking at it. In that way he fatigued very seriously the nervous elements as well as the muscles of the eye; and so the patient passed into a state of sleep or trance, from which Mr. Braid was able to obtain what are known as hypnotic phenomena. The older phenomena of mesmerism were brought about in a different way, by a person who was able to concentrate his will and his own magnetic force, throwing that force with all the strength of concentrated will on the person he desired to affect. He worked directly on the astral body by means of mental action; whereas the hypnotist works on the astral body by way of the physical, and so produces the bad physical effect, that by making artificial paralysis he fatigues the nerve and sets up unhealthy vibrations which tend to repeat themselves. Charcot always preferred to work on hysterical people, people with a tendency to epilepsy, and other forms of mental disease: those were the people most easily affected. He did not so much try to cure them, as to find out what results he could obtain from them, and the results were a further shattering of the nervous system as well as some exceedingly interesting psychical facts; but these facts were largely obtained at the cost of the physical destruction of human beings, a thing utterly antagonistic to all morality, and which ought to be condemned as a kind of human vivisection, even more wicked and more cruel than the vivisection of the lower animals. The results thus obtained you may read in many books that have been published. I shall only take a few samples to show the way in which by means of the astral the mind may work upon the physical body, and so bring about results which will lead us to our next part, the working of mind in forming images, and so later in moulding physical matter at its own will.

Take an ordinary hypnotic or mesmeric experiment. I should prefer mesmerism. Personally, I do not now use any of these experiments (I used to do them in my early days of investigation, before I knew the harm I might work), as I think, on the whole, they are mischievous. A person is thrown into a trance, and in that state he is told, say, that on his hand at a certain hour in the day will appear symptoms of a burn, that the skin will get red, that pain will be felt, that a wound will appear like a wound formed by a red-hot poker, and that all the symptoms, inflammatory and other, of a burn will be present. He awakes out of the trance, and so far as you are able to discover he knows nothing of what has occurred during that time. The hour arrives which has been fixed for this appearance; the skin begins to redden and pain is felt. The patient does not understand what is happening, but he is conscious that he is suffering pain. The symptoms become more acute; the skin gradually assumes an appearance which it would assume if touched by a poker, and you have a burn produced, not by external lesion, but by the action of mind, the mind of the operator working through the astral body of the patient, setting up there the image of a burn which then reproduces itself on the physical molecules, which, as I explained before, are shaped and moulded by the astral matrix in which they are embedded. If, when in Paris, you go to the *Salpetriere*, you can see a number of photographs which have been taken of burns which have thus been produced on the bodies of patients, and you may examine the doctors who have produced these lesions, and without external means have caused external injury.

This throws strong light on some so-called miracles. Where you have the production of what have been called the sacred stigmata — that is, the appearance on the hands and feet of the wounds of the Passion of Jesus — you are not face to face with a fraud, as many Protestants are apt to think, dealing with a Roman Catholic miracle. You are not face to face with a case of deliberate self-deception any more than a wilful deception of others. You are simply face to face with hypnotic phenomena produced in highly nervous subjects, such, say, as secluded monks or nuns who have their minds fixed constantly on one idea, who very often remain for hours in a single position with eyes upturned towards the Crucifix — in that very position in which Braid used to bring on his hypnotic trance. So are really produced these marks upon the physical body, which by those who believe them to be miraculous are looked on as endorsing a particular form of faith, while by those who hold another form of Christianity, they are regarded as deliberate and wicked frauds. They are neither the one nor the other. Like all miracles they are reducible under law; for a miracle is only the working of a law unknown to the people amongst whom the phenomenon occurs, and they, because they do not understand it, at once jump to the "supernatural", forgetting that, as the Divine is the source of all, there can be nothing which is not natural — there can be nothing outside and beyond the Divine nature and the Divine will. Take, then, that class of phenomena as interesting physically — interesting as showing that you can produce physical results without what we call a physical cause — a thing which fifty years ago science would have said was impossible, which fifty years ago would have been denounced as fraud, as it was denounced when brought about a hundred years ago by a man like Mesmer. Orthodox science denounced him as a charlatan and a rogue. The century that followed has justified Mesmer, and has made some of us fairly indifferent when science calls out "fraud" about other phenomena which we know to be as real and as natural as those which were denounced as fraudulent by the science of the eighteenth century, and are boasted of as modern triumphs by the science of the nineteenth. These, however, are the least interesting of such phenomena. Far more interesting are the mental workings on the mind of the patient — sending before his thought images produced in the mind of the operator, and so enabling him to see as an image that which only exists as thought in the mind of the controller.

But before referring to some of these experiments, let me give you an explanation from the standpoint of the philosophy I am trying to explain. I have spoken of the soul as the man. That soul when it works through astral matter on the brain is known as mind, for the mind is the lower manifestation of the soul — it is the soul embodied and active in the body, not the soul in its own nature, not the soul in its own sphere, not the soul which uses mind as well us body as instrument, but only the soul as it is seen and manifested in the brain — intellect, reason, judgment, memory: all those characteristics of the mind are qualities of the soul as the soul works through the brain. In its own sphere it works in matter of a much subtler kind, and there each thought is a thing. Every thought is a form; every thought has its shape in the subtle matter which is the matter of the soul-spheres. But when that shape is to make itself manifest to others who are living in the body, it must clothe itself in astral matter to begin with, and take a shape in which, in the trance or clairvoyant state, it can be seen as a form; then it may be projected further into physical manifestation. With that I will deal in a moment. Amongst those physical manifestations are some of the phenomena which have caused to much puzzlement in connection with the Theosophical Society in the minds of many both in the East and the West.

Let me take, then, with that brief explanation, the workings of the soul through the mind, the working of the mind on astral matter, and the proofs of it that you may obtain through mesmeric and hypnotic phenomena. Suppose you take a sheet of plain paper and throw your patient into a mesmeric trance. On that paper place a card smaller than the paper, and then trace round it with a little bit of wood an outline of the card. Say to the person who is in trance: "I will draw a line round the card, and you can see it". Then put the paper and the card away, and wake the person out of the trance. Apparently he will be quite normal, like you or me. Give him, then, half a dozen bits of blank paper, amongst which is the paper on which this imaginary line has been drawn round the edge of the card, and ask him if, on any of these bits of paper, he sees any figure. He will pass them over one by one, and when he comes to the paper on which this line has been drawn by the wood, he will say:" On this there is an oblong traced." In order to be sure that he sees it, ask him to fold the paper along the line he sees, and he will fold it along these "imaginary" lines that you cannot see. Then bring the card and place it on the folded paper, and you will find that he has folded along invisible lines so that he has the exact size of the card round which this "imaginary line" was traced, showing you that he sees this image that has been formed, and that it persists for him, his faculties having been thrown into this clairvoyant state.

Take another case rather more complicated. Here you want considerable concentration of will on the part of the operator. On a blank piece of paper throw an image. Take, for example, a watch. If you look at the watch it conveys a very definite image to your mind. Are you able in thought to project such an image on the piece of paper so that you can see it with the mind ? That is what is called visualising it. Some have great power in doing it. Every artist has the power to some extent. Every person can obtain it if he chooses to train his will and concentrate it. You can thus produce to your own mind a clear image, so that if you shut your eyes you can see the watch in thought. That is the condition of success in an experiment of this kind. Suppose I have my patient: I throw in my thought an image of the watch on the paper; that is, I fix my mind on the paper, and I see on it in my own thought an image of the watch. I need not speak a word, I need not make any sign or touch the patient; there shall be no contact between him and me; I will remain silent, and affect him by nothing except my mind. He shall then be awakened out of the trance. Some one else shall give him the bits of paper, so that there may not even be contact between my touch of the paper and his touch. Presently, looking over the bits of paper, he will come to the one on which my thought has made the image of the watch, and will say: "Here is a watch", Ask him to describe it? and he will describe it. Take it away, remove it to a distance until the outline grows dim, and he will say: "I cannot see it clearly". Now give him an opera glass, and the image will be recovered. Give him finally a pencil and ask him to trace over the lines of the picture he sees, and he will draw on that apparently blank paper the picture that you have made by your mind. What has happened?

The mind has in astral matter made the image by the force of its own thought, and that is visible to the person in the clairvoyant state. His astral body, which is active, vibrates in answer to it, and so by an inner sense he is able to see it. That is then transmitted to his physical eye, and he sees that which to the eye, not thus influenced, does not exist. But what is thus seen must exist, or it could not be visible under any conditions. On these matters Professor Lodge is making some interesting investigations. He has convinced himself that thought can pass from brain to brain by means of an idea being conveyed without any word or written expression at all. In all these experiments, case after case may be found by which you may convince yourself of the reality that thought, ideation, gives birth to form. But this may carry us very far. I have said that concentrated thought is necessary for such exact experiments, but it is not necessary for affecting to some extent the minds of others, which are all in nature like our own. Very concentrated thought is necessary to produce an astral image that another can see: comparatively slight thought is wanted to produce an image that another may receive in the mind. And so you come to thought-transference — another of man's powers familiar to every student of Theosophy, and now being investigated by modern science.

Before taking that, let me take the last stage of this production of images, which, I said, was connected with some of the phenomena which have caused so much curiosity and wonder and accusations of fraud in connection, especially, with Madame Blavatsky, the greatest wonder-worker of our time. It is a simple enough thing, this production of external material forms by a person who has trained the mind and the will. That means, of course, that the soul is sufficiently developed to be able to use the mind as an instrument — that which is thought to be impossible, I am afraid, in the western world. What happens is this. The soul in its own sphere strongly thinks, and produces a mind-image. That mind image, generated by the soul, is thrown down into the ordinary mind working in connection with astral matter. Then, into that mind-image is built astral matter—the molecules of astral matter — so that, as in the former case, it would become visible to the clairvoyant. But a stage further is possible. Out of the atmosphere in which in minute division, as you know, exists physical matter, minute particles of carbon, for instance, in the carbonic acid around us — those particles taken up by the plant and built into its own tissues — those tiny particles of solid matter are precipitated by means of a magnetic current into the form which has thus been produced by the action of mind on the astral matter. And thus a physical object is produced. The commonest form of this is the precipitation of writing. All that is necessary is that you should be able to think strongly each letter that you want to produce. You must make an image of the letter; you must then produce an astral image of that letter, so that, say, your letter A would exist in an astral form, held together by strong concentrated will. Then into that astral mould by a magnetic current, as easy to manipulate as the magnetic and galvanic currents used by your electricians when they precipitate silver from a solution on to the article they desire to plate — by quite as simple a process there is cast down out of the atmosphere the minute material particles which, in their aggregation, become visible: and then your letter A appears as precipitated on the paper. That is a description, stage by stage, of the production of precipitated writing. There is nothing miraculous about it; it is a simple process, as simple as any electric message, which, as you know, may be produced by writing on a tape by alternating currents which produce, if you desire, a facsimile of the writing of the operator at the other end. The difference between the working of the adept and the working of the electrician, is that the electrician wants an apparatus — a battery and a wire — to produce his result; while the adept uses the brain as his battery aud wire. For the human brain, as one of these adepts has told us, is a most marvellous generator of force, a most wonderful transmuter of mental into physical and physical into mental forces. There takes place the great alchemy of nature, and it can be governed by a purified and concentrated will. If you ask me: "Can I do it ?" I reply: "No, you cannot, because you have not trained yourself". Will you pardon me if I say what sounds very rude, that very few of you ever really think at all?

You drift. You do not think. You allow other people's thoughts to drift into your minds from the mental and astral world. The minds of most of us are nothing more than hotels into which drift the visiting thoughts that are in the mental atmosphere around: they come in for a bit, stay for a time, and drift out again — drifting in and out. So, men and women scarcely ever really think. Some minds are more like dust-bins than even hotels, and they put up a sort of label, " Rubbish may be shot here", in the form of the most trivial and ridiculous novels, the most frivolous and childish newspapers. Yet men and women who spend hours in that fashion, wonder that they cannot manipulate the forces of the mind, or use the power of the will which needs years of training ere it becomes ductile and obedient to the soul.

If you want to see whether I am judging harshly, try and think for one minute of a single thing, and before you have thought of it for half a minute the mind will be off on some other subject. Try and think of a watch for a minute after I have stopped talking, and before you have thought of it a quarter of a minute you will find yourself thinking: "What was it she said about it? How did she look when she said it? What was my neighbour doing at that particular moment?" Everything except the one thing of which you are trying to think. Then, perhaps, you will convince yourself, as I convinced myself by that very experiment, how very little power you have over the mind, how much you are at the mercy of outside thoughts, instead of using them as you yourselves please.

Or take another case. You have some great and pressing anxiety. You can do nothing at the moment; it will keep you awake all night. Why? Because it is your master instead of your mastering it. If you knew the life of the soul, if you understood the powers of the soul, you would never think of anything save that which you desired to think, and which you are using for some purpose. If you had coming on, say, some great law suit, and could do nothing to influence the result, you would not think of it until the time came: you would give your whole mind to other thought that was useful and spare yourself needless worry, which ages and kills far more than anything else. Let me say in passing that the power to do it is one of the great experiences which have come to us in the knowledge of eastern thought. For, at least, we have among the Hindus not great numbers who can do it, but great numbers who put before themselves that as an ideal, who know that it can be done, who realise the possibility, and who are the standing witnesses of this reality of the higher life of the soul, and the possibility of rising above body and mind into the true life where all causes have their place.

But even our careless thinking gives rise to forms; and this is a practical point of importance to us. As we think we create forms, and those forms are according to the nature of our thought, good or bad according as the thought is evil and evil-working, or good and good-working. The motive which underlies the thought governs the nature of the form to which we give birth; and that form when it passes out from us, passes into the astral world as a living thing, exists in that astral world influencing other people and forming part of the common stock of thoughts in the world. On this subject one of the great Eastern teachers has said:

Every thought of man upon being evolved passes into the inner world, and becomes an active entity by associating itself, coalescing we might term it, with an elemental — that is to say, with one of the semi-intelligent forces of the kingdoms. It survives as an active intelligence — a creature of the mind's begetting — for a longer or shorter period proportionate with the original intensity of the cerebral action which generated it. Thus, a good thought is perpetuated as an active beneficent power, an evil one as a maleficent demon. And so man is continually peopling his current in space with a world of his own, crowded with the offsprings of his fancies, desires impulses and passions; a current which re-acts upon any sensitive or nervous organisation which comes in contact with it, in proportion to its dynamic intensity. The Buddhist calls this his "Shandba"; the Hindu gives it the name of "Karma". [*The Occult World*, by A.P. Sinnett, Fifth Edition. pp 89-90]

That is what you and I are doing all day long, every day and week and year of our lives — sending out these currents of thoughts, peopling the mental atmosphere with our own thoughts, good, bad. and indifferent, thoughts of love and hate, thoughts of kindness and bitterness, thoughts that bless and thoughts that curse mankind.

Here is the creative region, here the greatest responsibility. I spoke of our power of physical creation: far more important is our power of moral creation; for as we give out thoughts, good or evil, so we affect our own and others' lives, so we build our present and our future, so we make the world of today and of tomorrow. What is the criminal? You and I think we can separate ourselves from the criminal, that we are so much better than he, not responsible for his acts, and responsible for his crimes. Are you so sure ? A criminal is a very receptive organism — passive, negative, with all the soil made by his own past thinking, that makes him easily attract and nourish every thought which is evil and cruel. But the soil will not bear bad fruit unless evil seed falls into it. How much of that evil seed do you and I contribute ? Perhaps some passing thought of anger, conquered a moment after, comes into the mind. That thought has gone out into the mental atmosphere, becoming a living thing, a force for evil. That force of anger going into the mental atmosphere of the criminal, falling into the soil prepared for it, will germinate as a seed germinates, and there it may grow, nourished by his own evil, into an anger which is murder, and is then condemned by the criminal law of man. In the juster law of the universe the generator of the angry thought shares the fault of the crime. Everyone who helps thus to pollute his brother is guilty of his brother's sin. So, also, with good thought. Every noble thought that we think goes out into the world as force for good, and, passing into some mind, whose soil is full of all good impulses, is nourished there into heroic action, and so comes forth as noble deed. Our saints and martyrs, our heroes and our thinkers, are ours in mind as well as by virtue of our common humanity. Our best goes to their making; our noblest goes to their helping. They are ours as we have helped to form them, and every thought we think of good goes to the making of the saint.

Such then, is some of the teaching of esoteric philosophy as regard man's nature and man's powers. Every one of us has thus a share in the making of the world; every one of us has thus a share in the building of the future. Today all that surrounds us is the outcome of past thinking; tomorrow our environment shall be the resultant of our present thought. Law everywhere; law in the mental and moral world as in the physical; but man the creator of his own destiny — man the builder, the moulder, the master of the world.

That, then, is the message which tonight I have striven to bring to you; that, the fragment of esoteric truth that I have tried to put before you. For thus it is that morality worked out in contact with philosophy finds its embodiment in life. Thus life becomes beautiful, life becomes strong, life becomes dignified, noble and serene. You and I as living souls have the future in our hands to model; ours the power, ours, therefore, the responsibility; for where the power is, there also lies the duty; and with the increased knowledge of power the duty and the responsibility increase.

www.ingramcontent.com/pod-product-compliance
Lightning Source LLC
LaVergne TN
LVHW041502070426
835507LV00009B/750